M000267753

Copyright © 2021 Estee Gubbay, Luxurist Travel, LLC

All rights reserved. No part of this publication may be reproduced, distributed, or transmitted in any form or by any means, including photocopying, recording, or other electronic or mechanical methods, without the prior written permission of the publisher, except in the case of brief quotations embodied in reviews, the worksheets at the end of the book and certain other non-commercial uses permitted by copyright law.

The information provided within this book is for general informational purposes only. While the author tries to keep the information up-to-date and correct, there are no representations or warranties, express or implied, about the completeness, accuracy, reliability, suitability, or availability with respect to the information, products, services, or related graphics contained in this book for any purpose. Any use of this information is at your own risk. All opinions expressed in this book are solely the opinion of the author.

Paperback: ISBN: 978-1-953806-06-2

Library of Congress Control Number: 2020922148

All photos available from Unsplash.
Interior design by Simon Thompson.

Salt Pier, Kralendijk, Caribbean Netherlands. Photo by Kris Mikael Krister

Contents

Oljato-Monument Valley, United States. Photo by Andrew Coelho

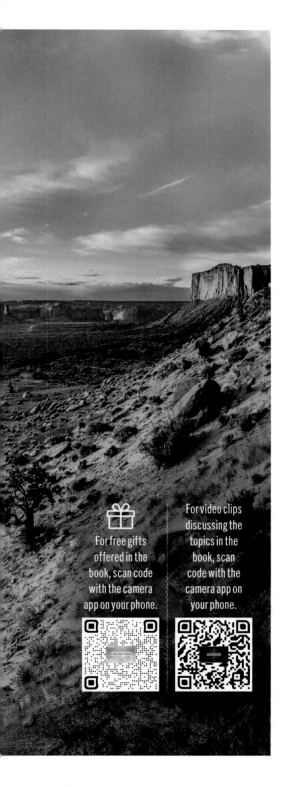

For free gifts offered in the book, scan code with the camera app on your phone.

For video clips discussing the topics in the book, scan code with the camera app on your phone.

Getting Started

1

"And then there is the most dangerous risk of all — the risk of spending your life not doing what you want on the bet you can buy yourself the freedom to do it later."

Randy Komisar

Iceland. Photo by v2osk

Introduction
Do you dream of rewarding travel?

Rainbow Mountain Peru, Cusco, Peru. Photo by Johnson Wang

RELAXATION

ADVENTURE

CONNECTION

PURPOSE

SELF-DEVELOPMENT

RENEWAL

> You want your travels to enrich your life and create the best memories - exciting, immersive, experiential, authentic trips where you learn and grow as well as relax and have fun. This guide coaches you to identify and celebrate these desires, so you can free them to be fulfilled. It's a combination travel guide, journal, goal planner, and self-development tool. With this process you will organize your wish list into a plan you can enjoy many years before the actual trips. I have taught this in countless workshops and to my clients, and I promise we will cultivate and curate every travel experience you have to be exceptional.

Your dreams are calling to you!

They're asking you to create plans and make them real. But without having the details in place, all you have are dreams which are mere intentions. Yes, you can travel without really planning, but those experiences can potentially fall short of what you've imagined. I know because it has happened to me!

When you look back on your past travels, ask yourself the following questions.

- Did you come home with the feeling of renewal?
- Did you grow as a person?
- Did you improve your life in any way?
- Did you develop a better connection with those you traveled with?
- Was your worldview expanded?
- Did you have an extraordinary experience? Or was your vacation a bit boring, underwhelming, and not what you had hoped?

I know it's frustrating to spend a lot of money on a vacation that is disappointing. Arguments can happen on trips because everyone doesn't agree on what to do for activities. The life experience you had hoped for doesn't pan out because no one learns anything new or goes out of their comfort zone on these trips. You just see the hotel and maybe some tourist spots and don't get out and experience the true culture of the places you visit.

Everyone wants to look back on a life filled with cherished moments they've shared with family and friends. But for many people, planning a lifetime of travel with such a high bar can be overwhelming. The big questions each of us face when we think about taking a trip to somewhere beyond our comfort zone are:

- Where do you start?
- Where do you go?
- How do you ensure these experiences will be special for everyone?

I know for a fact that many people plan trips based on popular destinations – those you see splashed all over TV and Instagram – and then come home a bit disappointed that it wasn't as memorable as they expected. What these sad travelers were missing — beyond a good travel advisor! - was a Travel Bucket List: a simple but effective long-term plan that motivates and guides you through one amazing journey to the next. With purposeful planning, you can create meaningful experiences and memories – the stuff that dreams are made of! Our leisure time is precious – on this I'm sure we all agree – so plan to make the most of it!

Your Travel Bucket List is for anyone with wanderlust (whether you are single or have a family) and who has big dreams for incredible trips. You may be just beginning to explore the world or planning travel in retirement. Maybe you have traveled quite a bit already and are looking for motivation to try something different. Have you vacationed in the same place several times because you enjoy it but you can't recall one vacation memory from the others? From now on, you'll create the greatest adventures of your life, produce more meaningful experiences and build extraordinary memories from your journeys.

If you like to be purposeful in your life, plan goals, dream big and take action in your life, you are in the right place. If these concepts are new to you, get ready to get out of your comfort zone. Together we will create a solid travel plan in which each trip will be unique and encompass your most important desires.

These are the first steps toward truly capturing your travel dreams, and mapping them out — so you can actually make them a reality!

The Gubbay Family in Portofino, Italy

Vernazza, Italy. Photo by Anders Jildén

"Twenty years from now you will be more disappointed by the things you didn't do than by the ones you did do. So throw off the bowlines, sail away from the safe harbor. Catch the trade winds in your sails. Explore. Dream. Discover."

Mark Twain

ADVISOR TIP
Have your travel advisor call ahead. Hotel managers are very open to leaving complimentary gifts in your room.

Agra, Uttar Pradesh, India.
Photo by Shan Elahi

There are many travel journals and books with suggestions of bucket list destinations, but this book is different. I teach that by first reflecting on your interests and what you desire from your trips, you can then choose destinations that have the best opportunity to achieve your desires. You are encouraged to plan well ahead and spark your creativity with the thoughtful journaling prompts, quotes, advisor tips, memory joggers and conversation starters provided. It's an easy read with inspiring true stories of other travelers that have enjoyed their bucket list vacations, as well as stunning visuals to give you new and unique itinerary ideas. As you complete the book, you will uncover what you love to do, create a travel style, and set the bar high with what you want to accomplish on your trips. The final worksheets help you set goals and create a tailored roadmap to achieve your travel dreams.

I hope you enjoy my unique perspective as a self-development coach and as a seasoned travel advisor and owner of Luxurist Travel Agency. (Before I was a travel advisor, I spent many years facilitating workshops on goal setting and pursuing a life of balance and fulfillment.) My clients include executives and high-profile business leaders as well as families, friends and solo travelers. I have the experience and knowledge to guide you through the step-by-step blueprint I use with my clients to get the most out of your trips and create truly unforgettable journeys with friends and loved ones.

I also walk the talk. I'm a dreamer, goal planner and go-getter. I've also traveled the world and curated enthralling trips with my own family and many others in just this way. My daughters, who are now young adults, are empathetic, brave, global citizens who care about learning and understanding other cultures and traditions. They believe wholeheartedly in being socially responsible. I believe that giving them opportunities to travel contributed to these traits.

More authentic types of experiences on your own trips will do the same for you and your loved ones.

Once you start this exciting process, you'll discover that visualizing and planning the trips you want to take in your lifetime is incredibly valuable in so many ways.

Dreaming and planning can be imaginative, expressive, and fun! You get a taste of your travels before they even begin, building up your anticipation and excitement! You stop living day-to-day and begin living trip-to-trip! With the right tools and guidance, the planning itself can be very rewarding. We are all familiar with the importance of goal setting to drive ourselves forward in life; why should it be any different with our travel bucket list?

You may already have a list of destinations you want to visit, but it's much more valuable to think in terms of what activities will excite you, and then find the best places to do them. Places where you can have unique experiences for growth, quality time, wellness and adventure. Adding this type of travel to your life fulfills you and reconnects you with yourself and the world around you.

The result will be a travel bucket list with a set of plans that encompasses who you are and what you truly love. These plans will carry you into the most pleasurable, memory-creating set of experiences you desire.

And my help doesn't end with this book. I have a wealth of information on my website and I'm always available to you for a free consultation. I can work with you individually and I can even create a custom travel portfolio. I use a new interactive tool and private travel portal that has thousands of travel experiences to get more inspiration for your bucket list. It saves time, money and most importantly, offers the peace of mind knowing you will achieve your travel dreams. This powerful combination of my expertise, supported by the latest advancements in technology and analytics, is a full service I offer my clients.

Get Started Putting Pen to Paper With an Exploratory Discussion

Block out some time. Sink into a comfy chair. Think about this:

Estee hosting a travel workshop

> **Why do you travel?**

Finding the answer to this question is especially important. Oh, and it's fun to discuss with others! When you feel that you've answered this question for yourself, think about it once more in the context of your traveling companions — they have their own answers to this question. You may also have a different answer if you travel with your family versus with a group of friends. Thinking about when you're all together is a key to what type of adventures you'll want to cook up. Talk this through with family and friends you want to travel with. It is a meaningful conversation, and you'll enjoy it. Obviously, if you are a solo traveler, then the expectations of others do not need to be considered. Instead, it's up to you to think about what motivates you to travel – what is your comfort zone and are you willing to step out of it?

I believe it's very useful for all travelers to think about why they travel. For those of you who are reading this guide, I'm sure your passion for travel goes far beyond simply "having a good time away from home." Discuss this with those you aim to travel with, whether on the phone or over dinner or a coffee. Unlocking their thoughts and dreams will help you plan the journey and quite possibly shine a light on your own travel dreams. By coming together to discuss your travel plans, you are exploring the type of adventures you all wish to experience. A meaningful conversation about a future journey can enlighten you to the possibilities ahead. Good communication is essential.

As you start contemplating the answers to the questions in this guide, you may experience some doubt if you will actually be able to go on these phenomenal trips. Fight this resistance and continue moving forward with your dreams!

People often have no idea what they would do if they had more time, for fear they will never actually be able to do it. This reflection process will connect you with the cherished moments you crave. Your work here is sure to inspire, engage — and make your travel experiences that much better.

Of course, you should be somewhat realistic as to what you are physically capable of doing, what your budget is, etc. However, since we don't know what the future holds for us, we can't be certain

Brainstorm
What sort of memories do you dream of building together with your traveling companions?

Photo by Ana Tavares,
Andrew Stutesman

Photo by Roberto Nickson

REFLECTION

What do you value when you travel?

Why?

where we may be financially or physically. Don't compromise yourself. Dare to dream a little bigger. Remember, you can always make changes as you plan your journey.

Don't be afraid to be creative. The journaling prompts are in this book to unearth latent desires and spark new ideas. Everything we do requires making creative choices. The greatest journeys start with a plan and then have the flexibility to explore options as they present themselves. Journaling is a powerful tool to access and express what might be dormant or a limiting belief. Allow yourself to be free of the worries about your ability to accomplish your bucket list. Impediments such as time, money, flexibility, ability, and determination will be overcome with good planning.

This is a tool for you to expand your mind to new possibilities. In the self-development world, this is a "growth mindset" rather than a "fixed mindset." This type of aspirational thinking is an effective way to create positive momentum toward your dreams and is essential to a happy life. Even the actual bucket list worksheets at the end of the book are not set in stone. You are not signing a contract to go on any of these adventures. You are making a proactive, fluid plan, which is so much better than waiting until you are desperate to get away, anywhere with the latest "best deal."

For many people, anticipating travel is a type of self-care. I've taught many workshops where we put together a Dream Board, a collage of pictures of goals, places and things we want to envision in our future. They work! Have you ever looked at a tropical beach screensaver on your computer and imagined you were there? It felt immediately relaxing, right? The positive feelings associated with looking forward to a trip are a great part of a self-care routine. This is soothing and can measurably reduce anxiety and stress. However, we have to do this mindfully, because it doesn't happen naturally.

If you are the lead family vacation planner, then

- ● **What have you dreamed of doing?**
  e.g., Parasailing
- ● **Why haven't you done it?**
  e.g., Scared
- ● **Without overthinking it, outline your ideal vacation day:**
  Morning - e.g., Yoga
  Afternoon - e.g., Snorkeling
  Evening - e.g., Dinner & Show
- ● **What is your most treasured travel memory?**
  e.g., Being part of a sunset drum circle
- ● **What experiences could capture some of the same magic?**
  e.g., Local festivals
- ● **Who are the people you travel with?**
  e.g., Friends that are couples
- ● **What do they value while traveling?**
  e.g., Socializing

FREE GIFT!
For a free, printable companion workbook, head over to
luxuristtravel.com/workbook

you should always be looking at several trips in the future. One of the things I recommend that you do is create a family travel bucket list. This will help keep the whole family inspired and looking forward to traveling together. Your children will be enthused when you ask for their input while your partner – even if they have told you to make all the decisions for the next vacation – will feel valued. Having given things some thought, he or she will likely come up with beneficial suggestions. Nothing is worse than going on a trip with a loved one who then complains, "I didn't ask for this!" If you have involved them in your travel bucket list they will, before you book your trip, have a clear idea of what is on offer.

Many of you will read this book and not do the journaling. You may say to yourself, "I've got the idea." If so, you are selling yourself short of a very enjoyable experience. So grab an empty notebook or print out my free workbook and start writing!

Find Out How You Like to Travel

"Life cannot be understood flat on a page. It has to be lived; a person has to get out of his head, has to fall in love, has to memorize poems, has to jump off bridges into rivers, has to stand in an empty desert and whisper sonnets under his breath. We get one story, you and I, and one story alone... It would be a crime not to venture out, wouldn't it?"

Donald Miller

Mount Tamalpais, United States. Photo by John Towner

Niche Travel & Personal Growth
What is your favorite type of travel?

> There are many different types of travel. Most everyone has done vacation travel, where you go to a resort, usually with a beautiful beach and sunny weather. Vacations are the ultimate way to relax, have fun and spend quality time by yourself or with friends and family.

Here I'll share a few of the other types I specialize in as a Virtuoso® community member. Within these communities, I receive advanced training and partnerships with select vendors who offer access to specific special offers.

These days there are all kinds of travel for the sophisticated traveler. What do you want to engage in during your leisure time? The list is very long and you can explore as many of these as you wish.

Choose which types of travel appeal to you and review the paragraph that corresponds to it.

- Personal Growth/Wellness Travel
- Celebration Travel
- Sports Travel
- Culinary Travel
- Volunteer Travel
- Adventure Travel
- Music Travel
- Ancestry Travel

Personal Growth/Wellness Travel -

This section focuses on experiences that restore a traveler's mind and body.

I'm a great believer in travel being one of the best occasions for personal growth. Many of you may well be aware of Elizabeth Gilbert's memoir *Eat, Pray, Love* where the author chronicles her travels across Italy, India and Indonesia in search of adventure, enlightenment and romance — plus great food. She managed to experience all of them and write a huge best seller! Well-planned travel and an openness to the new lands she traveled in ensured Gilbert could experience the personal growth necessary to recover from her bitter divorce, grow in wisdom and find love again.

Now Gilbert was already a very successful writer when she set off to travel for a year in search of personal growth. Not everyone can take a year off but many people do take a long weekend or a week specifically for this purpose. There are wellness resorts all over the world that include workshops, exercise and great food. My friends and I try to go to a different wellness resort each year. I plan many retreats as well, in which small groups embark on a trip with the specific purpose of slowing down, getting mindful, and reflecting on their lives. There are yoga retreats, couples retreats and self-development retreats held by trained experts in many beautiful "retreat centers" — destinations where only the retreat guests are there and you're not distracted by partying vacationers.

You don't need to take a whole week at a specialized resort to find many opportunities to

Leo Carillo, United States.
Photo by Kaylee Garrett

ADVISOR TIP
Niche travel is often organized by online travel clubs and anyone can join.

TRAVELER STORY

We have close friends that have six kids and travel often. They are luxury travelers but they always take a full day, on every trip to volunteer. How wonderful is that! They have made a lovely family tradition and taught their children to always be thankful for what they have and to give back. They are multiplying their positive impact as some of those kids are young adults now and planning their own trips to volunteer. Is this a tradition you can start with your family?

La Rosière, Montvalezan, France.
Photo by Matthieu Pétiard

experience wellness and personal growth: spend a few hours at the hotel spa, meditate on the beach at sunset or take a long walk. Simply taking the time to step outside your daily routine and focus on your self-care is most important.

You also have the opportunity to see how others live, how other cultures thrive and how there's beauty behind it all. This enhances your creative abilities by exposing you to things that are massively different from what you're used to experiencing.

There are so many ways that travel can enrich your life if you simply open your mind to it and take that first step on your own adventure. Use your intuition throughout this guide about what you need and what type of transformation you want in your life. Have a strong intent to widen your perspective and your travels will help you become a wiser person, give you a better understanding of your culture and others and grow your appreciation for your own life.

Celebration Travel -

Celebrating a special occasion is the perfect reason to travel. This category includes destination weddings, anniversaries, honeymoons, family gatherings, birthdays and more. Many times it comprises multigenerational families and event-planning services. Milestones are a wonderful time to plan these trips. Travel brings generations together and forges closer bonds. Also, traveling in groups of ten or more saves money. You can get a group rate at most hotels for 10 rooms and most cruise ships offer the eleventh cabin for free for the group host!

Sports Travel -

Popular sports trips can be organized by tour operators or you can plan trips yourself. Many sports clubs also offer trips. Groups often go as teams to compete in races, play in golf tournaments or go on ski trips, for example. You even can get VIP packages to events such as the Masters Tournament and to the Olympic Games. Several water-based sports also fall into this category such as fishing trips, scuba or sailing trips. Make sure your entire group is comfortable on the water!

Culinary Travel -

Also called epicurean travel, this features opportunities that go beyond traditional dining with well-rounded culinary experiences that are immersive, interactive and educational. These are typically luxury tours or cruises, but you can simply shop for your favorite foods in the country where they're made. How about having Belgium chocolate in Brussels? There are even programs to learn to be a chocolatier. Programs can feature a famous chef, offer cooking classes or hold tastings focusing on a particular region. Do you have a favorite chef you would love to meet in person? Do you have a favorite wine? Winery tours are part of this type of travel and an activity you can add to any budget vacation. It's a great way to engage with locals and see how they live. From a foraging camp in Sweden to fishing with a chef in Hawaii, home-style cooking in Fiji to fine dining in Tokyo, there are plenty of choices for your next food-themed trip.

Estee's daughter, Chloe at a cooking class in Tuscany, Italy

ADVISOR TIP

Many beach resorts have sea turtle conservation programs, where you can take part in a sea turtle release. Check for appropriate times of year.

Volunteer Travel -

For those who are passionate about helping others, there are many opportunities to volunteer while traveling. You can join a group like Habitat for Humanity and build houses, volunteer at an orphanage or help a village build a school or install a water purification system. If you can't take a whole trip for this purpose, there are many ways you can help during a regular trip. For example, many tours ask you to bring donations to drop off en route.

You can spend an extra day directly contributing to local conservation and conflict mitigation efforts. There are options to participate in community projects where human-wildlife conflict mitigation is the objective and will directly benefit local communities and the conservation efforts in the region. Guests can also choose to volunteer with endangered animals, with a desert elephant-tracking experience, a rhino or a lion conservation experience at an animal sanctuary, and more. Surely a life-changing journey like no other.

Adventure Travel -

This focuses on pursuits that include physical activity, a connection with nature, and exploration of unique cultural experiences. Specifically, it highlights experiences guests can participate in, not merely spectate. Adventure travel can involve going on safari in Africa, diving in a steel cage in shark-infested waters in the Pacific Ocean or trekking in the Himalaya. How about bungee jumping into New Zealand's pristine rivers? There are so many adventures to be had in our wonderful world that I could fill a book listing them all. Obviously, certain types are only suitable for able-bodied adults who are physically fit. But plenty of adventure travel is family friendly – safari parks in Kenya and Zimbabwe cater to families, and children love to see elephants and giraffes and myriad other animals in their natural habitats. By experiencing wildlife and conservation,

children grow intellectually and in empathy. Another great way to experience adventure travel is on an expedition cruise. Expedition cruising is much like traditional cruising, but with more emphasis placed on the experiences ashore, during excursions and in ports of call – many of which are much more off the beaten track than mainstream cruises. National Geographic partners with Lindblad Expeditions, where you'll explore alongside a dynamic expedition team — seasoned photographers, marine biologists, historians or naturalists. Flexibility is built into each itinerary, so that you can take advantage of wildlife sightings or other spontaneous opportunities that arise. These nimble expedition ships can navigate narrow waterways and small harbors that larger vessels cannot reach, and they're equipped with exploration tools such as kayaks or paddle boards, snorkeling gear, Zodiacs, hydrophones and underwater cameras, so that you can discover wild places close up. If you would like a more luxurious adventure cruise, companies such as Silversea offer them too. This is a great way to see Alaska, Antarctica, or the Galapagos Islands on a small ship.

This type of travel doesn't have to be extreme or occupy all of your vacation time. Take an afternoon on your beach vacation to go zip lining or ride some ATVs. Discover some hidden cenotes in Mexico or walk across hanging bridges over the La Fortuna waterfall in Costa Rica. This is a wonderful way to challenge yourself and have an amazing, unforgettable experience.

Ancestry Travel -

Also called DNA tourism, genealogy tourism, or heritage travel, ancestry travel is a trip taken to explore places of special significance to your family's history. With the availability of at-home DNA testing kits and ability to search for long lost relatives on the Internet, many people are planning these types of trips. By discovering your cultural roots in the cities, towns and villages where your ancestors once lived,

The Gubbay Family on ATV's in the Arenal Volcano Area, Costa Rica

Burning Man 2013, Black Rock City, United States. Photo by Angie Corbett-Kuiper

it's easy to feel connected. Visit the heritage sites, enjoy the cuisine, experience the art in the area and make friends with the locals.

If your partner – or family members – aren't quite as excited as you are to engage in ancestry travel, then you should emphasise all the other delights they will experience when traveling to your chosen destination: Ireland has the world's best pubs. Italy has lovely lakes and villages. Ukraine has historic cities and a stunning coastline. Great travel involves engaging, learning, experiencing and returning home with memories you will never forget. Ancestry travel certainly achieves all these.

Music Travel -

Americans pioneered the music festival with Monterey and Woodstock in the late 1960s, but it was the British who developed it to an entirely new level: Glastonbury Festival, in the West Country of England, is the world's most popular music festival, with around 300,000 people attending and millions more watching the live broadcasts on the BBC. Not far from Glastonbury is the farm land on which Peter Gabriel's Womad Festival is held every July – this is a remarkable gathering of music and dance from across Asia, Africa, Latin America and beyond. You can hear Malian griots and Cuban crooners and Moroccan rappers and much more across one weekend. Coachella Festival, held in Indio, California, is the world's most chic festival with influencers and top pop stars, models and movie stars all lining up to be seen there. Burning Man in the Nevada desert is surely the craziest, artsiest music festival on earth, but they don't like to call it a festival — it's a community wherein almost everything is created entirely by the participants, who are active in the experience. Tickets are hard to get and sell out fast. You also need to be willing and able to camp for a week in the desert. It's a very welcoming, creative, party atmosphere with sculpture installations, theme

Glastonbury Festival Site, United Kingdom. Photo by Joe Green

camps and techno DJs as well as live music.

If you are thinking these festivals all sound far too youthful and energetic but you do love music, consider a reserved music festival. There are festivals for classical music, soul music, jazz, folk music, bluegrass, country music and much, much more. Some may be huge but many are small, often only hosting a few hundred people. New Orleans hosts more music festivals than any other city in the United States. They are held right in the central districts so everyone can stay in a hotel and can walk to the venues. A new addition in terms of comfort to festivals is the rise of "glamping" — luxury on-site camping. Glastonbury, Womad and Coachella offer this. That said, Burning Man festival remains resolutely hardcore and demands its revelers to camp in the desert without access to even the most basic luxuries — one for adventure travelers!

Think about what activities excite you! The world offers up many unique experiences for growth, quality time, wellness and adventure. Listen to your desires. Plan what you want to do, and go about making your travel experience uniquely yours. Don't settle for less.

REFLECTION

What new ideas for trip themes have come up for you?

Pinpoint Your Travel Style

> There are many different kinds of travelers, from those who love adventure and entering uncharted territories to those who prefer heading somewhere they feel comfortable, in a place where they can simply relax on a beach with a drink and not be confronted by challenges. You may want to experience "slow travel," a term which is any type of travel that encourages you to slow down. For example, you might get a one-way ticket and plan to stay a long time in one or more areas, discovering the local culture in an authentic way. You may be more of a vacationer — one that travels to get a break from work and be catered to for a week or so. You also may already be accustomed to a certain quality of service and accommodations that are considered "luxury travel." Don't worry, there is no right or wrong way to travel! You may want to mix it up. So let's firstly consider some of the different types of traveler styles.

ADVISOR TIP

Small group, jet tours can save you as much as 14 hours of time in airports and are the ultimate first class experience.

Hop on board the Four Seasons' brand new luxury plane

Image by falco from Pixabay

River Cor

ESTEE'S EXAMPLE

I planned a 30th anniversary trip for a couple who had never been to Europe. They hadn't done much traveling and had no idea what type of travel appealed to them. The wife had been doing tons of research on every country, hotels, tours, etc. She was overwhelmed! I suggested a cruise. At first, they worried they wouldn't get to see much or have authentic experiences with locals. That's just not the case. Now, cruise companies make a point of offering lots of different excursions, extra nights in ports and pre- and post-stays. The couple was able to visit six different countries in one trip! Also, cruise ships vary widely in size and class. Usually, the smaller the ship, the more luxurious the service. But even less expensive, mainstream lines offer more luxurious cabin categories, with private dining, butler service, private lounges and many upgrades. Even if you travel with a group that has wildly different tastes and budgets, staying in different cabin categories can allow you all to go together. Put the kids in an interior or attached cabin and splurge on a large, veranda suite for you! You can all meet up or hang out in the suite's living room during the day.

WHAT IS GLAMPING?

Glamorous camping, which is the combination of camping or various other eco-conscious accommodations with some of the amenities and luxuries of a hotel room. It's a type of experiential travel that connects with nature in a more authentic way.

EcoCamp Patagonia, Torres del Paine, Torres de Paine, Chile. Photo by Jonas Dücker

What style of travel appeals most to you?

- Do you want a guide on your trips?
- Do you like to travel independently?
- Do you like guided group tours?
- Day activities with a guide?
- Private guided tours?

How do you want to get from place to place?

- Do you like river or ocean cruises?
- Trains?
- Sailing?
- Yachts?
- Cruise ships under 1,000 passengers?
- Expedition ships?
- Mega cruise ships?
- Private jets?

What about the accommodations?

- Stays hosted by a local?
- Boutique hotels?
- Large resorts?
- Glamping?
- All-inclusive resorts?
- Private houses?
- Branded hotel chains?

What type accommodations do you like?

- e.g., All-inclusive resort

What quality?

- e.g., 5 stars

ADVISOR TIP

An advisor can often get you upgrades that can take your accommodations from 4 to 5 star.

What Experience Do You Have as a Traveler?

> **Your level of experience traveling starts on your first trip and changes as you go through life stages. What stage you are in can dictate a lot about how you may choose to travel.**

Choose your level of travel experience and scan down to the paragraph that corresponds to it.

- New traveler
- Seasoned traveler
- A traveler who has not traveled much in a long time
- Young family traveler
- Experienced family traveler
- An empty nester or retirement traveler

Are you a new traveler?

Are you just starting out as a traveler? Maybe you've done a little travel with your family or have taken a few trips on your own – but you feel that you would like to venture farther and experience new destinations. Like so many of the great challenges and opportunities in life, travel requires you to step out of your comfort zone, take chances, experience new lands and meet new people. And you know what? You will love it!

Think of first experiencing travel like this: When we were children at the swimming pool or water park, many of us were initially scared to go down the big water slide or jump off the high diving board. We hesitated and wanted to climb back down to the safe, firm, dry ground again. But finally we held our nerve, and off we went – down the slide or off the diving board. And it was awesome! From that first time on, it became easy to do. The little bit of fear when going to a water park is part of the fun and now you can spend an entire day laughing and enjoying different water rides. Travel's like that. It can initially seem daunting. But once you have experienced traveling you too will want to do it time and again. The thrill and adventure of going to a new place and having new experiences will light up your mind, body and soul. So what do you want to be like in the future, and how do you want to grow as a person?

Are you a seasoned traveler?

If so, you have likely taken plenty of vacations – possibly in many different locations. But, do you ever get the feeling that your travels are not as rewarding as they possibly could be? Have you vacationed in the same place several times because you enjoy it, but your vacation memories tend to blur together? You might remember the

"The greatest legacy we can leave our children is happy memories."

Og Mandino

Lahbab Desert Safari, Lahbab, United Arab Emirates. Photo by Atlas Green

Oxbow Bend at Grand Teton National Park, USA. Photo by Stephen Walker

different times you went, but struggle to recall how one vacation stood out from the others. If any of the above rings true, then now is the time to reawaken your vision: Travel is among the most amazing experiences we can enjoy on earth. And your leisure time is precious. Don't waste it! Do something different! Think about how you can plan travel that fulfills your dreams, awakens your senses, stimulates your mind and encourages you to continue evolving as a person. This is the travel that builds lasting memories while inspiring you to achieve greatness in other areas of life.

If you've tended to travel a lot to the same familiar places, you might hesitate at the uncertainty of trying something new. But remember, you can stay with the same hotel chain or cruise company that you're comfortable with using. You know what the quality and style of the experience will be. But you can still travel to many different places! You can also get rewards for being a faithful customer, such as special club lounges or upgrades.

Are you a traveler who has not traveled much in a long time?

When the Covid-19 pandemic started, everyone had to cancel their trips. It took six months before people were going anywhere! Once the Centers for Disease Control started lifting the travel bans, road trips became very popular. After that, when more and more countries started opening up to travelers, everyone looked for fairly short flights because they didn't want to wear a mask for too long on a plane. The effect on the economy made it hard for many to feel comfortable even leaving a deposit for a future trip. We all had to take a break from planning the big

> "Be careful who you make your memories with. Those things can last a lifetime."
>
> **Ugo Eze**

bucket list trips for a while. You may now feel a little nervous venturing out again and traveling too far from home.

Work and family commitments often stop even the most passionate traveler from traveling far. But now, with all the new sanitation guidelines, you're ready to get back on the horse (or on the cruise ship). You now may dream of traveling in greater comfort and, perhaps, with new interests in culture or cuisine? All this is possible. It doesn't matter whether you wish to travel again to the great European capitals you once lit up as a college student or to seek out new, experiential travel. Putting in some journaling time here will help you with your planning, allow you to build upon your knowledge and ease you back into traveling.

There is a bit of a new learning curve to traveling now. Keeping track of what each country's requirements to enter is a full-time job. (I know because as a travel agent, I get notifications all day.)

Don't worry too much about this. I'm just a call or email away if you want professional advice.

Are you a young family traveler?

Are you someone who, for several years, traveled either solo or as a couple, but now you have children to bring along? If so, then you now need to approach travel with a somewhat different mindset. Traveling with children is not as difficult as you might imagine: Kids are great travelers, always interested, full of energy, quick to make new friends. You don't have to worry about them enjoying themselves – they will! What you do have to consider is how to plan a family vacation that ensures everyone in your family will have the opportunity to do things they want to do. You don't want to drag your kids around to places they don't want to be. Excursions and activities you do have to be age appropriate. For example, you should be aware of their ability to pay

attention on long museum tours or how long they can last on a hike on a hot summer day. You want to be sure to add some exposure to locals and regional culture. Depending on their age, you might want to give them a little more freedom than at home. Being on a cruise ship can be great for this. There are lots of activities for all ages, and they are within the confines of the ship.

You and your partner will surely want some quality time where it's just the two of you. You might want to look into planning a vacation where a degree of child care is provided – huge numbers of hotels and resorts now offer all kinds of activities that keep young bodies and minds engaged. Some even have baby day care or your own nanny available. Your kids can make lifelong friendships at these kids clubs — mine have. Many resorts have their own cultural centers or wildlife preservation centers with educational activities for all ages. Think about which vacation experiences will provide enduring memories for your children: Whale watching off Victoria Island? Climbing up the active volcano on Stromboli, a tiny island off Sicily? Trekking through the rain forest in Guatemala? These are just a handful of the many wonderful experiences families can enjoy together while traveling. Believe me, a well-planned vacation with the family builds bonds and creates lasting memories – it is worth its weight in gold. I've been there: My two daughters accompanied my husband and me on trips from an early age. They will both tell you that the experiences they had traveling as children are their favorite memories and helped shape them into the well-adjusted, open-minded, inquisitive and daring individuals they are today.

ADVISOR TIP
Plan your travel outside of school holidays and summer. It is much less costly and destinations are less crowded.

Are you an experienced family traveler? Do you often take your trips as a family?

Something I learned early on as a mom who loves to travel with her family is this: You can get more adventurous and travel farther as they get older!

There's no need to stick to the family-only resorts once they are in their teens. When you can trust them to be good guests and go off on their own (within the confines of the resort), you can book adult resorts, where you can hang out with your spouse at the adult pool. Don't go on the group tours where families are shepherded around a handful of obvious tourist sites, jumping on and off the tour bus, without any real engagement with the local culture. These tours tend to be rushed and done without a great deal of thought: Often they will include lunch at a place you wouldn't choose on your own, then back on the bus with your guide reciting the same tired jokes he (or she) reels off everyday as you head for another pit stop at another historic monument. At the end of the day, everyone returns to the hotel, tired from sitting all day in traffic on a bus – sometimes there is a traffic jam of tour buses as they all try to reach the same site! Children and teens can be grouchy, strapped into a tour bus seat for hour after hour while being lectured and, when back in the hotel, rush to return to their iPads and phones, oblivious to the world outside. Splurge on a private tour instead. Your family can have one custom planned for what you want to see. Then, if you're not enjoying a stop on the tour, you can move on to another any time you want.

A great family vacation should be stimulating, unforgettable and also relaxing: I know as a parent how nice it is to be able to relax with (or without) your kids, to get to the novel you've been wanting to read, practice yoga, get the deep tissue massage and facials you have been holding out for, use the gym for a long workout, sleep late, not have to rush or cook or clean. Believe me, it's possible to do all this while traveling and have happy children!

Marina del Rey,
United States.
Photo by Tyler Nix

Magelang Rafting Elo River, Desa, Dusun 1, Progowati, Magelang, Central Java, Indonesia. Photo by Angga Indratama

A lot of growing families rent vacation homes. I owned and managed a luxury beach house rental for many years. I can tell you the mom (even if it was a multi-generational family and she had adult kids with their own children) ended up still feeling like she was on the job on these types of trips. You do all the planning, a lot of the cooking, and even still clean up after everyone because housekeeping doesn't come back until the end of the week. Forget about the convenience of having a kitchen, or at least hire a cook and daily housekeeping!

When my family stayed in Fiji, our resort villa came with a full-time butler/housekeeper/cook, a nanny for every child under the age of six and a buddy to do daily activities with children from the ages of six to twelve.

I've encountered many clients who are disillusioned after spending a lot of money on a vacation that ends up being exhausting. They come to me as a travel advisor and, after initial pleasantries, express their frustration at how much they spent on the last trip only to find their children – or the entire family – bored and disappointed. And when a family is stuck in a hotel or a resort and boredom/disappointment takes hold, then disagreements and arguments inevitably break out. You definitely do not want that sort of thing when you go on vacation.

A great trip with older children is one where they learn by stepping out of their familiar environment. Trying new things and growing in confidence together as a family strengthens the bond you have together. And, as parents, you know nothing is more rewarding than witnessing your kids enjoying themselves and growing as individuals. If your children are happy and engaged, then you also are likely to be so. Do take some time to share the bucket list exercises in this guide's companion workbook with them and invite them in on the planning of your future travels. They may already have dreams of what they want to do and where

they would like to go and come up with some remarkable ideas! If they love to read and watch TV and movies set in different parts of the world, then they may be looking forward to exploring new lands. Traveling as a family is one of the greatest bonding experiences possible. Dream big, plan well, and you will surely find that your family – parents and children – arrive home stronger and happier. Successful family travel is one of the best investments possible, providing both an education impossible to get in school and experiences that will secure lasting family memories.

Are you an empty nester or retirement traveler?

As a travel advisor I often encounter new clients who speak with great joy of their travel memories – sometimes undertaken as children with their parents, other times as college students who used summer vacation to seek out new lands and adventures. Quite often couples have traveled extensively before settling down to raise a family. As children leave home and/or retirement frees up time, many people decide that they would like to return to traveling, and take longer trips. But things have changed since they stopped traveling so frequently. Perhaps you are also very different from your younger traveling self? Did you once stay in youth hostels and go to the late night bars and clubs in every major city? Fun as those backpacking days were, I understand that you may not want to return to them.

How do we make the most of travel now? And how can we get the biggest bang for our buck? You may wonder if you are still capable of traveling now that you're older. Of course, just as you might not feel safe cycling in the traffic like you once did, you may not want to plan an open-ended trip where you don't know if you have a bed to sleep in every night. Also, if it's just the two of you, do you secretly worry you will be bored? Don't worry. Travel offers a vast

Estee's in-laws, Bill and Cheryl overlooking Lake Lucerne, Switzerland

ton of money and miss all the crowds and young families. If money is not really an issue, you can even own your own cabin on The World, a private yacht and luxury vacation residence in one. It's the largest private residential ship on the planet and home to only 165 residences. An international community of residents and guests spend extensive time exploring the most exotic and iconic destinations, and return onboard to a lifestyle that exists nowhere else on earth. That's my retirement goal!

Alternatively, if you have plenty of spending money but not much time, jet tours are now very popular. They cost what some people make in a year but save travelers an average of 13 days in transit compared to taking commercial flights. Most of these ultra-luxury tours are between 14 and 25 days long; you can travel extensively through a region or around the world on custom-configured jets (with about a fourth of the amount of seats on a standard jet). Groups are between 15 and 50 guests, depending on the size of the jet. This is first class all the way with 5-star hotel stays and small group itineraries. Experiences are designed just for you and have insider access, such as skipping the line at museums, after-hours gallery tours and private musical performances. You can even arrange for an exclusive dinner in a temple or a privately chartered train to a natural wonder like Machu Picchu. Everything is custom and all inclusive. My goal is to take a jet tour like this before we buy a cabin on The World! You only live once!

array of opportunities for all different interests and enthusiasms. Even the most niche interests are catered to. The bucket list examples in this book will help you imagine the possibilities.

Did you know that living on a cruise ship can cost less than a senior living community? It's true! I know several older adults who go months at a time on a single cruise ship. They venture all over the world on back-to-back itineraries or world tours. All cruise ships are wheelchair accessible and have medical doctors on board, daily housekeeping, restaurants, shopping and tons of shows and activities. It's a retirement dream! And this is not just for older adults. If you have the freedom to go where you want at off-peak or shoulder season times – when everyone else isn't on vacation – you can save a

"Travel is still the most intense mode of learning."

Kevin Kelly

ADVISOR TIP

Many tour and cruise companies are now offering exclusive trips for families and millennials.

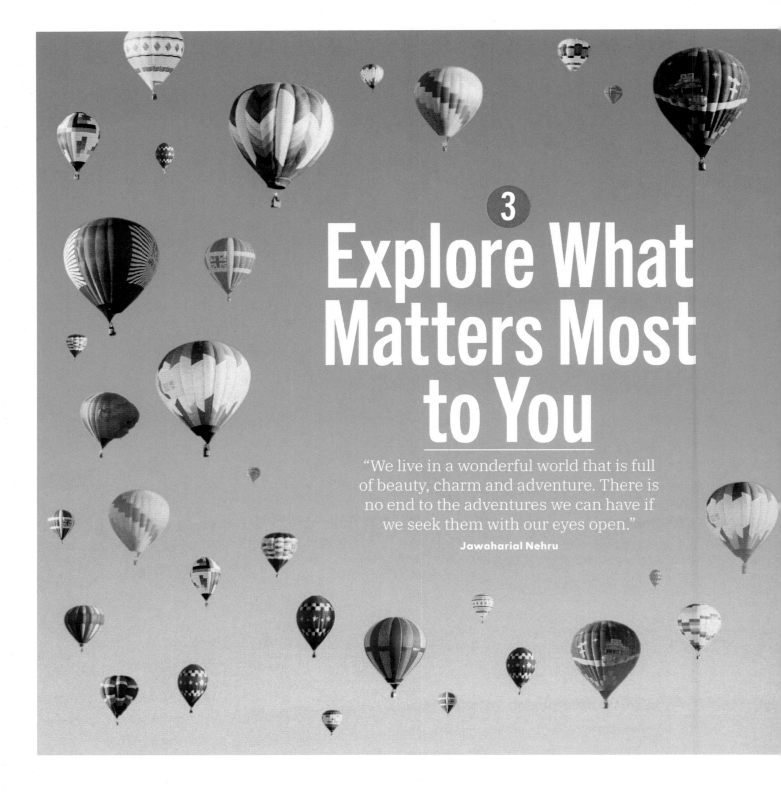

3 Explore What Matters Most to You

"We live in a wonderful world that is full of beauty, charm and adventure. There is no end to the adventures we can have if we seek them with our eyes open."

Jawaharial Nehru

Albuquerque, United States.
Photo by Ian Dooley

"Remember
to celebrate
milestones as
you prepare for
the road ahead."
Nelson Mandela

Identify Your Milestones

Milestones mark progress on a journey.

> Your milestones are the events on your life's path that are meaningful to you. These milestones make for wonderful opportunities to travel, because all the meaning they carry feeds into the memory-making power of the trip.

Do you think of any birthdays as milestones (18th, 21st, 30th, 40th, etc.)? Do anniversaries or graduations serve as milestones for you — or others that you'll be traveling with? How would you like to celebrate these? Perhaps you'd love to send your high school graduate to Europe on a teen tour. Maybe you dream of spending your wedding anniversary in Paris, or your 50th birthday at a wellness resort. You might entertain visions of swooping your entire extended family on a spectacular vacation for your 70th birthday. List your life milestones that you would enjoy planning around.

Your personal and family milestones:

- **Name**
  e.g., me
- **Milestone**
  e.g., 50th birthday
- **Date**
  e.g., January 12th

Photo by
Victoria
Priessnitz

ESTEE'S EXAMPLE

I have planned all of these trips and more for my clients. For my own family, I sent my husband and daughters to Washington, D.C., for college tours. We timed the trip around late November, which allowed them to visit my husband's mom for Thanksgiving dinner. I took the same week to celebrate my milestone birthday and jumpstart my fitness with a wellness week at the Golden Door Spa in California. I had been dreaming of going to that luxury spa for many years, and the "big" birthday justified the indulgence.

ADVISOR TIP

Ask your travel advisor to arrange a photographer to capture your memories with a photo shoot at your destination.

Questions to Stir Your Imagination Even More

The right questions can inspire your imagination.

> Here's a great list of questions to help you stretch your imagination about the types of places, activities and experiences that will create the best memories for you. Discuss them over coffee with a friend or at the dinner table with your family.

Estee's daughter, Makayla snorkling in Kona, Hawaii

1. You're starring in a movie, one with amazing cinematography; what spectacular scenes do you envision yourself in?
2. How are you different one year after your next trip — spiritually, emotionally, and physically? (What changes in your life would you like to see after returning from a trip?)
3. Your family sits around a holiday dinner, laughing and reminiscing about a shared vacation experience; what was that experience?
4. On a long-awaited vacation with your significant other, you take a deep breath and feel gratitude for the moment you're in, and the fact that you're with that person. Where are you, and what is that special moment?

REFLECTION

Write your responses to the relevant questions.

Neuschwanstein Castle, Schwangau, Germany. Photo by Eric Marty

"Don't tell me how educated you are, tell me how much you traveled."

Mohammed

WHAT ARE UNESCO WORLD HERITAGE SITES?

World Heritage Sites are protected cultural and/or natural sites considered to be of "Outstanding Universal Value." Many are areas of exceptional beauty and have a historical, scientific or other form of significance. Places as diverse and unique as Stonehenge in England, the Pyramids of Egypt, the Great Barrier Reef in Australia, the Galápagos Islands in Ecuador, the Taj Mahal in India, the Grand Canyon in the USA, and the Acropolis in Greece are examples.

Stonehenge, Salisbury, England, UK.
Photo by Mitch Hodge

What Are Your Interests and Hobbies?

Do you want your travel to be an authentic and immersive experience unlike any other?

> Every few years you should take stock of what you find interesting when you travel. This is an important step! Your interests will grow and change. By first taking your current interests into account, you can choose the best locations to experience them.

Example Interests

- Culture
- Food and wine
- Geography
- Shopping
- Wellness
- Meeting Locals
- Water Sports
- Music
- Land Sports
- Nature
- History
- Art
- Animals
- Fishing
- Festivals
- Castles
- Architecture
- Scenic Views
- Volunteerism
- Meditation and Yoga
- UNESCO World Heritage Sites

TRAVELER STORY

I know a father and daughter who had a hard time planning vacations. When I asked them about their hobbies, they couldn't come up with any. They said they were too busy with work and school to take on any other activities. I asked what they do for fun when they need a break. They said that they just watch TV. Then, they mentioned that they are big fans of the show Survivor. We planned two trips out of this. One trip to Los Angeles, to be guests at a Survivor Finale Show, and one to Fiji, to stay in the Survivor US filming location and home of the crew at the Mana Island Resort. These trips brought their downtime to another level!

Brainstorm

Have a discussion of common areas with your traveling companions. If you have children, are there particular values or strengths you would like to help them cultivate?

Plan your trips around these themes.

This makes your trips so much more meaningful and interesting! Sure, you will have occasions where you just go somewhere because someone invited you or you found a great sale or want to check out a few destinations on a cruise. This will all be fun and can be added to your bucket list as they come up. The key to this guide, however, is to plan the most inspiring, unique adventures that help you grow as a person, open up new opportunities and create unique memories that are special for you!

REFLECTION

- What are your current interests?
- What are your hobbies?
- What types of trips do you like? ski, beach resort, european tours, expeditions?
- What new activities would you like to experience?
- Do your interests change based on your mood?
- For example, sometimes you might like adventure and other times you might prefer R&R.

ADVISOR TIP
Safari tours often combine immersive cultural and volunteer experiences.

The Teen Giving Club at San Miguel Home, Guatalama

ESTEE'S EXAMPLE

My oldest daughter founded a volunteer club in high school called The Teen Giving Club. She and her friends were (and still are) passionate about volunteering with disadvantaged youth and inspiring other teenagers to volunteer. As a part of their work, they spent a year fundraising for a Guatemalan orphanage. Afterwards, we planned a week-long trip for 15 club members to stay and facilitate activities at the orphanage. I included a weekend of fun activities on Lake Atitlán to enjoy after the volunteer experience. They went zip-lining down the side of a volcano, learned about natural medicine, were taught how to color fabric with plant-sourced dyes, how to weave and more! Most importantly, their time at the orphanage bonding with the children was life-changing. While there, they filmed a documentary to teach other teens how to create their own nonprofits. Their documentary lead to opportunities to talk about teen volunteerism at local schools and it also won the San Diego Leadership Award. My daughter now works as a non-profit consultant while in college. This trip is a prime example of how travel can help people expand upon their passions and create positive change.

Marrakech, Morocco. Photo by Tom Tiepermann

Amsterdam, Netherlands.
Photo by Sabina Fratila

Which Activities or Experiences Will Create the Best Memories?

 Planning your travel dreams is all about choosing experiences that create memories.
What hobbies do you have or want to cultivate? What kind of memories do you want to gather? What do you want to learn?

Example Experiences

Animal-Related
- Become scuba certified and swim with manta rays, sharks, or dolphins all over the world
- Play with a monkey
- Feed and wash an elephant
- Go on a safari to see the Big Five

Festivals and Events
- Go to festivals
- Witness the Olympic Games
- See the cherry blossoms blooming in Japan
- Attend a yoga or wellness retreat

Culture
- Try new foods in their original country
- Learn how to cook from a famous chef
- Go to a famous museum
- Have a walk-on role in the Sydney Opera House in Australia
- Browse books at the Livraria Lello store
- Attend a West End or Broadway show
- Learn about wine tasting at a beautiful winery
- Go on a genealogical tour and trace your roots

Outdoor Adventures
- Zip line over a volcanic lake
- Hike to a famous peak
- Learn to snowboard
- Take a helicopter to an ice cave
- Repel down a waterfall
- Go to a summer camp or ranch for families
- Jet ski on a turquoise lagoon

Memorable Sites
- See the Seven Wonders of the World
- Tour villages where Game of Thrones was filmed
- Take a ferry around Sydney Harbor
- Visit a UNESCO World Heritage site

Volunteerism and Conservation
- Help build an orphanage
- Release baby sea turtles into the ocean
- Work on reforestation projects
- Teach English or a skill

REFLECTION

What are your ideas for activities and memory-making experiences?

The Ancient Wonders of the World

1. Great Pyramid of Giza - Giza, Egypt
2. Hanging Gardens of Babylon - Ancient Babylon, in current-day Iraq
3. Colossus of Rhodes - Rhodes, Greece
4. Lighthouse of Alexandria - Alexandria, Egypt
5. Statue of Zeus at Olympia - Olympia, Greece
6. Mausoleum at Halicarnassus - Bodrum, Turkey
7. Temple of Artemis - Izmir, Turkey

The New Wonders of the World

1. Great Wall of China - Huairou District, China
2. Petra - Ma'an, Jordan
3. Machu Picchu - Peru
4. Chichen Itza - Yucatán, Mexico
5. The Colosseum - Rome, Italy
6. The Taj Mahal - Agra, Uttar Pradesh, India
7. Christ the Redeemer - Rio de Janeiro, Brazil

The Seven Natural Wonders of the World

1. Rio Harbour - Rio de Janeiro, Brazil
2. Great Barrier Reef - Queensland, Australia
3. Grand Canyon - Arizona, USA
4. Mount Everest - Nepal and China
5. Victoria Falls - Zambia and Zimbabwe
6. Paricutin Volcano - Michoacan, Mexico
7. Northern Lights (also called Aurora Borealis) - Alaska, Iceland and other locations

Surely, of all the wonders of the world, the horizon is the greatest."

Freya Stark

TRAVELER STORY

I helped a family to book a 70th birthday celebration trip for their mom. She loved to cook, but with four adult children living in different cities, it was hard to have big family meals or spend time in the kitchen with the grandchildren. Together, we created an experience for all 16 of them on an all-inclusive vacation in Cancún. Most importantly, we included a group Mexican cooking class and dining experience for everyone to participate in together. The mom was thrilled! The pictures of them all wearing aprons with straw hats and rolling tortillas are priceless! Can you see what I mean here about creating memories?

WHAT ARE THE SEVEN WONDERS OF THE WORLD?

The ancient "Seven Wonders of the World" were categorized by Philo of Byzantium in 250 B.C. and, since then, just saying the "Seven Wonders of the World" is no longer specific enough. There are the ancient wonders, natural wonders, and even engineering wonders of the world — and the list changes often.

South Dakota, United States. Photo by Stephen

Docile whale sharks.
Photo by Michael Liao

ESTEE'S EXAMPLE

Here's a list I created in 2015, with my dream activities and their accommodating destinations. Since then, my family and I have done them all and more!

- Scuba with sharks in Fiji
- Rappel down a waterfall in Arenal, Costa Rica
- Swim in a cenote in Cancún, Mexico
- Shop for leather bags in Italy
- Experience the very best chocolate in Belgium
- Stroll the tulip gardens in Amsterdam

Choose Destinations That Match These Activities

> **This is the first time in the process that you are brainstorming destinations.**

You have a lot of suggestions in the book, but you may need to do some research or talk to a travel advisor. Keep an open mind! There may be places you have never heard of or previously considered going to. And remember, you are not searching for the most popular or trendy destinations; you are seeking locations known for the experiences and the activities that you seek, ato properly build those fantastic memories!

ADVISOR TIP

An On-site is a local company that works exclusively with travel advisors to provide insider experiences.

"One's destination is never a place, but a new way of seeing things."

Henry Miller

TRAVELER STORY

A business graduate school student wanted to learn about his Jewish heritage during his summer break. While on a tour of Israel, he found a free entrepreneurship program for the following summer in Tel Aviv. (Fun fact: Israel has more venture capital per capita and more start-ups than any other country in the world.) He applied and got started on his business there. Now, a few years later, he has his own successful start-up!

• To see a short video of our shark dive, go to
www.luxuristtravel.com/blog/fiji-family-dive

Where Else Do You Want to Go?

> **Here's your opportunity to get all those destination dreams down on paper.**

Now you can write down all those places you have heard about or seen on TV and in movies ... places you know you want to visit.

Estee's husband and daughter, adventuring in Arenal River, Costa Rica

REFLECTION

- What are some places you definitely want to see?
- What places do you need to research more?

ADVISOR TIP

When choosing destinations, be sure to consider the weather. Off-peak season might be when it's not the best weather.

Machu Picchu, Peru. Photo by Willian Justen de Vasconcellos

"If you reject the food, ignore the customs, fear the religion and avoid the people, you might better stay at home."

James Michener

4

Refining Experiences

"The purpose of life is to live it, to taste experience to the utmost, to reach out eagerly and without fear for newer and richer experience."

Eleanor Roosevelt

Salar de Uyuni, Uyuni, Bolivia. Photo by Christopher Crouzet

Have Your Family and Travel Buddies Do the Same Exercises

 Yes, this is your list, but there will be times when you travel with others.

If you have kids, find out their interests. They may surprise you! The same is true of friends with whom you may travel, and even your significant other. The only limit to what you may discover is your curiosity and interest. Ask questions, practice active listening, pull on every thread.

I've given you space in the companion workbook to take notes from others, but they may want to spend some time reflecting on their own. Encourage them to add to your answers or fill out their own workbook.

Some of us may not have suitable traveling partners right at hand. If you have goals to go places and you don't know anyone else who is interested, many apps and websites can help you meet other like-minded solo travelers. Or you can go on a group tour. As a travel advisor, I travel solo a lot and always meet other solo travelers who end up becoming friends. Don't be afraid to travel solo ... it can be a very liberating and self-realizing experience!

Plan a boys' trip or girls' trip. Encourage your friends to take a weekend away to do something you all enjoy. Many groups tend to gravitate to travel that includes physical activity and achievement, like golf or surfing. Others commonly seek leisure and socializing,

like wellness resorts and winery tours. Maybe you have a group of friends, book club buddies, a church group or sports team with similar interests.

Go back to your list of traveling companions and your shared preferences. If you are planning trips with them, include a diversity of places and activities to allow each person to experience something they are passionate about. Consider their top place picks, favorite types of experiences and activities, fitness levels, budgets and everyone's schedules.

Brainstorm
What preferences do you share with your traveling companions?

ADVISOR TIP
Your travel advisor can appoint you as your group's trip host and your travel is free!

ESTEE'S EXAMPLE

When my younger daughter was 12, she became passionate about saving sharks from extinction. So, for our next vacation, we prepared by taking family scuba certification classes. Then we went to Fiji and scuba dived with bull sharks! And not in cages! It was an area in the ocean called "The Bistro." Huge containers of tuna were there. Dive masters hand-fed the sharks like dogs with treats, while we stayed behind a short wall of coral.

That was not only a fantastic way to keep my daughter interested for several months, but also to show her how far she can go with an interest — and how brave she can be. Since then, our family has chosen many trips based on what type of marine animals we can swim with! Our trips have taken us snorkeling with dolphins in Maui, scubaing with giant manta rays in Kona, Hawaii, playing with stingrays in Bora Bora, barking with sea lions in La Jolla, California, swimming alongside whale sharks in La Paz, and much more.

Kargi, Kenya.
Photo by
Ian Macharia

Lapland, Finland.
Photo by Simon Smith

"Do not follow where the path may lead. Go instead where there is no path and leave a trail."

Ralph Waldo Emerson

Top Bucket List Activities and Their Destinations

> You have spent some quality time reflecting and brainstorming on activities that are the most important to you and you have matched a few of them with destinations. Now I'm going to share with you a very large list of activities and my suggestions for the best places to do them.

See if any of these match destinations you have picked. There might be a destination you haven't considered or don't know of yet. This is where it gets exciting! Take time to discover these new areas so that you can make the best choices for where to go on your trips. Try doing online searches such as "Where are the most beautiful fjords of the world?", "What are the top cycling destinations?" or "Where are the best places to see endangered animals?" Then ask your travel companions to do the same with what you're interested in. Do any of these appeal to you?

Activities and Experiences

- Horseback riding on the beach in Mexico
- Feeding stingrays in a lagoon in Bora Bora
- Hiking the Grand Canyon, USA
- Riding a camel in Petra, Jordan
- Wine tasting in France
- Glamping and a Big Five jeep safari in Africa
- Staying on a river cruise up the Danube or Rhine River, in Western Europe
- Cycling in Amsterdam, Holland
- Riding a helicopter over an active volcano in Hawaii
- Swimming in a cenote (cave pool) in the Yucatan Peninsula, Mexico and Belize
- Biking down Haleakala Crater in Maui, Hawaii
- Observing penguins on expedition in Antarctica, New Zealand or South America
- Kayaking or stand-up paddling on Lake Louise in Alberta, Canada
- Cruising in a luxury, small ship in the Caribbean
- Chartering a yacht in the Mediterranean Sea
- Pretending to be a Navy Seal for a day (with Trident Adventures, Hawaii)
- Helping baby turtles reach the ocean in Hawaii or Mexico

Oceano Dunes SVRA, Oceano, United States. Photo by Austin Neill

Danco Island, Antarctica.
Photo by Derek Oyen

- Jumping or repelling down a waterfall in Dominica in the Lesser Antilles of the Caribbean Sea
- Dog sledding at a ski destination (There are many great areas for this.)
- Staying at a ranch in Montana, USA
- Exploring a glacier ice cave in Whistler, British Columbia, Canada
- Scuba diving with bull sharks in the Beqa Lagoon in Fiji
- White-water rafting in Fiji or the Grand Canyon, USA
- Scuba diving with giant manta rays in Kona, Hawaii
- Snorkeling with dolphins in Kona, Hawaii
- Soaking in the mineral-rich Blue Lagoon in Iceland
- Skiing with a beautiful mountain view in Aspen, Colorado or Wegnen, Switzerland
- Seeing the world on a jet plane tour
- Taking the Game of Thrones scene tour in Dubrovnik, Croatia
- Learning to cook Italian food in Italy
- Scuba diving in Great Barrier Reef, Queensland, Australia

- Sailing on Halong Bay, Vietnam
- Taking a train trip through Switzerland and stopping at the top of Jungfraubahn
- Trekking the Annapurna Circuit in Nepal
- ATV adventuring in Mexico, Hawaii or Costa Rica
- Zip lining in Arenal and Monteverde in Costa Rica
- Shopping at the floating markets in Damnoen, Saduak District in Thailand
- Strolling the souks of Marrakech, Morocco
- Sleeping in a hotel made of ice in Jukkasjarvi, Sweden
- Cruising the Nærøyfjord in Sognefjord or the Geirangerfjord in Norway
- Driving across the world's most elegant bridge, above Øresund, between Sweden and Denmark
- Seeing a Broadway musical in NYC or a West End musical in London, England
- Taking a romantic gondola ride in Venice, Italy
- Having lunch on a cliff in Cinque Terre, Italy
- Going to a beach club in Ibiza, Spain
- Hot-air ballooning over Cappadocia, Turkey
- Seeing the Asaro Mudmen of Papua New Guinea
- Taking a sunset catamaran cruise to see the colors of the Rivière Noire in Mauritius
- Swimming with whale sharks in La Paz, Mexico
- Hiking at "God's Window" viewing point over Blyde River Canyon in South Africa

Scenic Places
- Lake Louise in Alberta Canada
- Mount Fuji In Japan during the cherry blossom season
- Iceland's Northern Lights
- The Great Wall in China
- Namibia, Africa by safari, especially at sunset
- The Grand Canyon observation deck or a helicopter ride over the Grand Canyon, USA

ADVISOR TIP
Teens love Alaskan expedition cruises because they are so interactive. Zodiac & kayak excursions let them connect directly with nature.

Bondinho do Pão de Açúcar, Rio de Janeiro, Brazil. Photo by Davi Costa

Cairo, Egypt. Photo by Omar Elsharawy

Brainstorm

Ask your traveling companions if any of your most appealing activities and destinations also interest them.

- Bora Bora's overwater bungalows facing Mount Otemanu
- A villa in Tuscany, Italy
- The famous blue dome church on the coastline of Santorini, Greece
- The waterfalls of Plitvice Lakes National Park in Croatia
- Salar de Uyuni salt flats (when wet from rain and reflective) in Bolivia
- Machu Picchu, Peru
- Vinicunca Rainbow Mountain, Peru
- The Arches in Los Cabos, Mexico
- Uluru, also known as Ayers Rock in Australia
- Iguazu Falls in Argentina and Brazil
- Mont Blanc in Switzerland
- Kauai's Na Pali Coastline, Hawaii
- Torres del Paine National Park in Chile
- The Seven Scenic Lakes in Patagonia, Argentina

Estee's husband, Paul Gubbay on the Superman Zipline in Playa del Carmen, Mexico

Famous Venues and Monuments

- Western Wall in Jerusalem, Israel
- Gardens of Alhambra in Grenada, Spain
- Keukenhof Garden Tulip Fields, Netherlands
- Palace of Versailles in France
- The Colosseum in Rome, Italy
- The Acropolis of Athens, Greece
- Statues on Easter Island
- Sydney Opera House and Bridge, Australia
- Taj Mahal in India
- Sphinx pyramids of Egypt
- Eiffel Tower in Paris, Frace
- Big Ben and the Houses of Parliament in London, England
- Walt Disney World, Florida, USA
- Smithsonian Institution, Washington, D.C., USA
- Metropolitan Museum of Art, New York, USA
- Louvre Museum, Paris, France
- Stonehenge, Wiltshire, England

Famous Events and Festivals

- Holi "Festival of Colors" in India
- Running of the Bulls in Pamplona, Spain
- The Christmas markets in Vienna and Budapest
- The cherry blossom festival in Japan
- Burning Man in Black Rock Desert, Nevada, USA
- Carnival in Rio de Janeiro, Brazil
- La Tomatina in Valencia, Spain
- Harbin International Ice and Snow Sculpture Festival in Harbin, China
- Mardi Gras in New Orleans, Louisiana, USA
- Día de Los Muertos in Mexico
- King's Day in the Netherlands
- Oktoberfest in Munich, Germany
- The Coachella Music and Arts Festival in California
- St. Patrick's Day Festival, Dublin Ireland
- Loy Krathong Celebration of Light and Lanterns in Thailand
- Songkran Water Festival in Thailand
- WOMAD (World Of Music, Arts & Dance) in Wilshire, England
- FES Festival of World Sacred Music in Morocco

"Drink heavily with locals whenever possible."
Anthony Bourdain

Get Inspiration From Others

> **Feeling like you've run out of new ideas?**
> Once you have exhausted your ideas for experiences, you can keep your eyes out for other sources of inspiration:

- Social media, websites, travel guidebooks
- My blog - luxuristtravel.com/blog
- TED Talks - ted.com/
- Travel TV channels - travelchannel.com/
- Travel magazines, like Virtuoso Life® (contact me to get this magazine for free!)
- Virtuoso Wanderlist® - luxuristtravel.com/wanderlist. For my VIP clients, This is an online social program where travelers can get hundreds of ideas, create and share their travel wish lists and curate a full travel portfolio.

Warrior dancer in Tahiti, French Polynesia

Ayers Rock – Uluru, Mutitjulu, Australia. Photo by Danny Lau

"Because in the end, you won't remember the time you spent in the office or mowing your lawn. Climb that goddamn mountain."

Jack Kerouac

REFLECTION

What are your go-to sources for travel inspiration?

"Don't be afraid to ask for help when you need it. Asking for help isn't a sign of weakness, it's a sign of strength. It shows you have the courage to admit when you don't know something, and to learn something new."

Barack Obama

Lake Louise, AB, Canada. Photo by Chen Ling

Consider Professional Support for Building Your List and Plan

> **Some people find the very idea of a list to be daunting.**

Your list is supposed to be deeply personal and meaningful. It's intended to launch you on a series of life-fulfilling experiences ... you might be intimidated by the prospect of taking on such a project all by yourself.

That's one wonderful way in which an experienced and travel-wise professional can support you.

A good travel advisor collaborates with you to design your whole travel portfolio. I love coaching my clients on their travel dreams. As I mentioned in the introduction, my background as a mastermind

TRAVELER STORY

I have a family in San Diego, California, that has been to Cabo San Lucas, Mexico and Maui, Hawaii, more times than they can count! The trips were all fun and relaxing, but their kids can't decipher which trip certain memories belong to. They are all blended together. I finally got them to plan a trip to Costa Rica, where they enjoyed many unique, adventurous activities. They rafted on the Arenal River, for example, the first time they had ever been on a river. They also had their pick of tubing, rappelling, horseback riding, waterfall jumping, hiking, taking a boat safari and more. When I work with my clients on their travel plan, they discover new travel ideas using an amazing, private online travel portal filled with videos, articles, music and activities from around the world. Then we meet in person or by video conference to discuss their results and brainstorm trips that match everyone's desires and interests. To cap off the experience, I give them a gorgeous wooden travel portfolio, filled with all of their information, survey results, budget, maps, a travel trip sequence and schedule.

Khlong Hae Floating Market, Thailand. Photo by iSAW Company

group facilitator and self-development coach makes me uniquely qualified to do this! Let me also point out that clients who do not have a long-term travel plan typically go to the same places every few years. They habitually wait until two months or so before the trip to plan, don't have time to do sufficient research, and then just pick the easiest choice of destination rather than the most exciting or memorable itinerary.

A good travel advisor is so much more than a booking agent. They spend time getting to know you and your travel style and what you want to do or accomplish on your trips. You don't know what you don't know. Travel advisors typically have specialties and are experts in particular types of travel and they are able to curate

> "We live in a wonderful world that is full of beauty, charm and adventure. There is no end to the adventures we can have if we seek them with our eyes open."
>
> **Jawaharial Nehru**

unique experiences with vetted travel companies that you can't find on your own. And now with the whole world at our fingertips, it is so confusing and time-consuming to plan a trip online. You need advice!

Back before the Internet, travel advisors were called travel agents because they mostly booked trips out of catalogs. They were typically employees who didn't travel much on their own. These days, most of us are in our own businesses, and everything we need is online. We have greater independence and freedom to do our own travel, and we define areas of particular expertise.

Many travel agencies work as independent contractors with large host agencies and a consortium.

WHAT IS A TRAVEL CONSORTIA/CONSORTIUM?

A travel consortia is a member-only group that can include travel agencies, host agencies and travel suppliers. Consortia can deliver huge volume and negotiate with hotels, resorts, cruise lines, and other suppliers on behalf of their agent members. The resulting "preferred supplier" relationship benefits agency clients in the form of upgrades, room amenities, and special promotions not available to the general public.

This is a big benefit to the traveler as these large companies have contracts which save you money, get you valuable additional upgrades and amenities, and in general give you more clout than if you are one traveler on your own.

Some good questions to ask a travel advisor before committing to them would be to ask what their speciality is and if they work with a particular consortium such as Virtuoso®, Ensemble®, or Signature®. My consortium is Virtuoso®, which specializes in luxury travel. Your advisor may also have additional preferred vendor partnerships through their host agency that translate into better deals for their clients. But most importantly, your travel advisor should want to get to know you and put that extra effort into making sure your trips are exceptional.

Whether you decide to DIY your travel plans or use professional help, the basic process is similar: Fire up your imagination. Get your creative juices flowing. Once you're inspired, challenge yourself to define your goals and plans in even greater detail.

Petra, Jordan. Photo by Emile Guillemot

5
Final Touches

"If you can dream it, you can do it."

Walt Disney

Lake Kawaguchi, Fujikawaguchiko, Japan. Photo by Daniel Hehn

Festival of colours.
Photo by Jasbeer Singh

Name Your Travel Bucket List

 Pick a name that will inspire you every time you see it.

First, let's stick with happy, positive names. "Stuff I Need to Do Before I Die" just won't do. Yes, this is a bucket list, but the point of the list is to live your life to the fullest! The emphasis is on living a fantastic life with lots of meaningful travel. A few starter ideas are provided below:

Examples

- Our Dream Travel List
- My Life Travel Goals
- Lifetime Travel Planner
- My Mindful Travel Journal
- Our Ultimate Travel Planner
- Family Adventures Around The World
- Places to Go in My Lifetime
- Our Lifetime Journeys
- Amazing Experiences To Be Had

"I never travel without my diary. One should always have something sensational to read in the train."

Oscar Wilde

Find a Place to Keep Your List

The Gubbay Family in Florence, Italy

> "Your brain will work tirelessly to achieve the statements you give your subconscious mind. And when those statements are the affirmations and images of your goals, you are destined to achieve them! "
>
> Jack Canfield

> **If you don't write it down...then it's not a list.**
It's possible that you already have an organized system for keeping track of all the moving pieces of your life, including various lists. And, in today's world, it's likely these files exist digitally on your computer or phone. However, your travel bucket list should have a special place of its own. The best way to do this is the old-fashioned way, with paper. Writing a list on paper represents a commitment that produces results, not just hopeful thinking. Like a dream or vision board, keeping your goals in front of you keeps them top of mind, solidifies your ambitions, and motivates you to achieve them.

So far you have comprehensively and uncritically expressed and recorded your thoughts and ideas about travel. But you don't need those notes in your actual travel bucket list. You need to simplify your brain dump to be specific and narrowed down to plans that appeal to you the most.

Put your list somewhere accessible, so you will be able to review it easily. If you like, you can copy and print the back pages of worksheets in this guide or download my free worksheet PDF file and put them in a binder. Adorn the cover with an inspirational quote or pictures of activities you've included on your list. Or copy the pages into a scrapbook with your own embellishments. Make it beautiful and put it right on your coffee table along with this guide for further inspiration.

Be organized with this! As you get further into the exciting process of planning your travel dreams, your list will develop into something much more than a simple, one-page document. It will be detailed, meaningful, goal-oriented, and inspiring. I'd suggest a goal of about 10 trips. You can always add, remove, or change things on your list as your interests change. As you change.

ESTEE'S EXAMPLE

I have had a list like this since college. I put it in a picture frame on my desk so I could see it every day. It's helped me be successful in many ways. The first item on my list was to plan a spring break trip with my friends to Cancún. One day, I came across a flyer from a travel company that was looking for college students to sell and host this exact trip! I posted flyers all around NYU for an informational meeting and invited all my friends. I took 12 students with me on that trip — and my roommate and I went for free! That was the beginning of my travel career!

Grand Canyon, Arizona, USA. Photo by Westwind Air Service

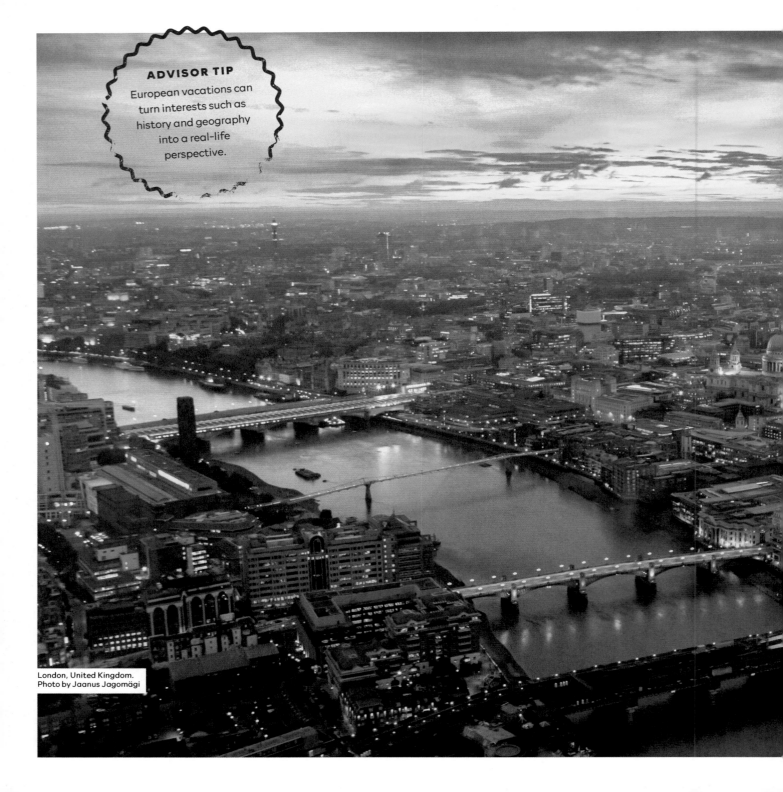

ADVISOR TIP
European vacations can turn interests such as history and geography into a real-life perspective.

London, United Kingdom.
Photo by Jaanus Jagomägi

Turn Your Bucket List Into a Solid Travel Plan!

 Get it done and enjoy the process!

Set aside time for this, because it's truly one of the most rewarding parts of the process. Sit down with a cup of tea to contemplate, or have a family meeting. Just by making the list, you will learn so much about yourself, and anyone else who'll join you on your travels!

Everything you're writing down is headed for your Master Bucket List Worksheet. When you are ready to transfer your ideas onto these sheets, this will be your Ultimate Travel Bucket List! Filling out these Trip Plan Worksheets is the final step in planning your lifetime of journeys! All you need to get there are the details!

FREE GIFT!
Download your free Master Bucket List and Trip Plan Worksheets at luxuristtravel.com/worksheets

Create a Schedule
Setting a date begins to make it real!

The Gubbay Family in Whistler, Canada

 Now is the time to go back to your milestone list and other important dates.

Consider those milestone dates. Next, look at holidays, work or school vacations. Do you want to plan a ski trip each winter? How about a summer vacation around the Fourth of July? Is there a week that you don't have to work that is not during a peak holiday season?

Next, look up the peak, shoulder, and off-peak seasons for your destinations. At the same time, you will want to take into consideration the weather. Peak seasons are generally during summer and school holidays, and will cost more and have less availability, but usually have the best weather and an array of activities. If you are free to travel during shoulder seasons (the ones in between peak and off-peak), you can have the best of both.

Another important consideration might be the dates of festivals. You may want to celebrate with the locals or find a quieter time to visit that destination. Sporting events can be a great way to enjoy a new country, such as going to a soccer game (or futbol, as they call it) in Spain. The Olympic Games obviously draw travelers from all over the world and it's an exciting time to travel to the host destinations, but you have to plan well in advance.

What milestone dates are coming up for you and your traveling companions? Would any of those make a nice time for a trip? Check with your traveling companions and see if they can commit to traveling. This part can take forever if you let it. Set solid boundaries about when you expect them to pick dates, and focus only on the dates at this point. You can talk about destinations and budget later.

Brainstorm
What are some other travel dates that fit your criteria?

REFLECTION

- What are some candidate milestone dates for your trips?

- Do you need to travel during holidays? Can you go off-season? How many trips do you want to take each year? How about some weekend trips or a sabbatical? What are some travel dates that may work for your traveling companions?

- Both in your workbook and on a calendar, write down dates that will work, creating a tentative schedule:

Sydney Opera House, Sydney, Australia.
Photo by Johnny Bhalla

"The road is there, it will always be there. You just have to decide when to take it."

Chris Humphrey

Acropolis, Athens, Greece. Photo by Francesca Noemi Marconi

Decide on Your Destinations

> **You've narrowed down When. Now do that for Where.**

Choosing the location of your trip comes after you research what you want to do. Don't be too quick to list the obvious tourist destinations! Take some time to study what places in the world offer the best versions of these activities. Review some of my lists for suggestions, ask friends, and do some research online. It may be that nearby a popular tourist area is another, less known (and less crowded) location that provides a more authentic experience.

Here are some examples.

Cancún, Mexico has been very popular for many years, but nearby Playa de Carmen is a step above. It has the newer resorts, on bigger properties with better beaches. Every adventure activity theme park you can imagine is there, as well as a permanent venue for a Cirque du Soleil show. If this sounds too commercial for your taste, you'll want to venture to nearby Tulum. Tulum has been gaining ground as the hippest destination in the Yucatan. There, you will find ancient Mayan ruins, retreat centers, local restaurants and several luxury boutique hotels, including many that are eco-friendly. The jungle is right alongside the beach, and you can find treehouse-style accommodations and even over-water bungalows.

Also popular in Mexico is Puerto Vallarta, but for the most stunning beaches and resorts, head 45

Tuli Wilderness, Botswana.
Photo by Matt Artz

minutes away to the newly developed area, Punta Mita, or a little farther to the very authentic surf town of Sayulita.

Great Barrier Reef is the world's largest coral reef system, but the Mesoamerican Barrier Reef is the second largest barrier reef in the world and the largest coral reef in the Western hemisphere. It spans 625 miles along the coast of Honduras, Guatemala, Belize and Mexico.

In the United States, many people visit Los Angeles, and you may want a day or two there, but the really lovely beaches and towns are south of L.A. Laguna Beach in Orange County has the most beautiful coastline, fine restaurants and art galleries. Instead of flying into L.A., you can go

directly to San Diego, where I moved to pursue a permanent vacation lifestyle. This is called "America's Finest City" for a reason! The downtown boasts the historic Gaslamp Quarter, which includes Petco Park and several blocks where nightlife spills onto the streets. There is also the Embarcadero, with a beautiful convention center. Seaport Village is right on the harbor, where you can stroll during the day, or catch the trolley to Balboa Park and the San Diego Zoo. Further north are many wonderful beach towns, all with a different feel. Go to La Jolla for shopping on Avenida de la Playa and for dinner with a cliff-side ocean view, or walk along the coast

> "People travel to faraway places to watch, in fascination, the kind of people they ignore at home."
>
> Dagobert D. Runes

to see the sea lions. At La Jolla Shores beach, a boardwalk leads to the sand and a protected marine underwater park, where sea life abounds. You can learn to surf, paddleboard, scuba or take a kayak tour of the cliff-side caves.

Maui is the most popular island in Hawaii, but there are also fantastic experiences on the Big Island. Stay near Kona to swim with dolphins or scuba with giant manta rays. Take a helicopter tour of an active volcano and see lava flow into the ocean. Take a crater rim drive and encircle the active Kilauea volcano in Hawaii Volcanoes National Park.

If you are looking for the ultimate Mediterranean trip, consider one of the islands off of Spain. Ibiza is famous for its nightlife, but nearby and more family-friendly Mallorca also has gorgeous beaches and hillside villages that rival Italy. In Palma de Mallorca, the capitol, you can wander narrow cobbled streets with elegant archways, grand historic palacios, medieval churches and charming squares.

REFLECTION

What are your top location picks? Map out the next three to six travel possibilities.

● To see a short video of our manta ray dive, go to www.luxuristtravel.com/blog/manta-rays

Photo by Marcin Ciszewski

WHAT IS A BOUTIQUE HOTEL?

A boutique hotel is a unique, small and intimate hotel, typically with a stylish design or themed decor. They usually have between 10 and 100 rooms, and can range from affordable to luxurious. They distinguish themselves from larger, chain hotels by means of their cultural or historical authenticity, and they provide interesting, unique, and personal services.

Pick a Variety of Lodging and Types of Travel

 You've made some real progress on your plan ... keep going!

Each trip you plan may be different and it's fun to travel in a variety of ways. Now is the time to go back to your lists and pick a few favorites. Remember that nothing is set in stone ... but it helps to plan!

Lodging -

There are many types of lodging. I recommend trying several in your bucket list. For beachfront vacations, I recommend the larger resorts with plenty of amenities or all-inclusive resorts. For cities and towns, I recommend boutique hotels.

You can also rent a house or villa, which can give you greater privacy but are available on many larger resorts. This gives you the benefit of lots of space and your own kitchen, but all the amenities of a hotel. You may even get your own golf cart to get around the property.

If you love the ocean you can stay in an overwater bungalow, charter a live-aboard boat, or stay in a river or ocean cruise ship. Keep in mind that overwater bungalows typically cost more than typical rooms on a hotel property and usually require a walk to get to the main beach and other hotel areas. River ships typically are styled like boutique hotels, have about 100 guests and come in all price ranges and levels of service. Ocean cruise ships can vary greatly in size and classification. I prefer the smaller, higher end cruise ships of about 300 to 1000 guests because they are more luxurious, can get into smaller marina's that the larger boats can't and are much faster to embark and disembark when in port. Many enjoy the larger, more mainstream cruise ships because there is so much to do on board while at sea.

FIT -

FIT, "flexible independent travel" are leisure trips without an escort or fixed package structure. The components of the itinerary may resemble a package, but the itinerary is custom-built for the traveler.

Tours -

There are other ways to enjoy several areas within one trip, with or without a group. Aside from cruises, there are also bus, train, jet tours, and private or group tours. I suggest private tours so you can be more in control of what you see and do.

ADVISOR TIP

River cruising is the most convenient way to enjoy several destinations. The small ships keep everyone together, you only unpack once and they are all-inclusive.

REFLECTION

For each destination that you have chosen, pick a travel type, such as FIT or tours, a lodging preference and a level of service.

Fill Out Those Worksheets!

It's all coming together!

Cheerful Sinulog dancers. Photo by Herbert Kikoy

> **Are you ready to review your journal and workbook and make some further choices?**

All the notes and brainstorming you have been doing with this guide mean very little if you don't take the next step to narrow down all that information to a selection of trips. This isn't a process you will do in one sitting, but make sure you get started on your actual travel bucket list! It doesn't have to be a finished product and of course you can make changes at any time. Think of it like a journal you can go back to with new ideas. In these worksheets, you will write your destinations, activities and dates but, more importantly, you will reevaluate why you want to do each trip, what you would like to learn and which memories you hope to create. You will choose your traveling companions and consider what you need to do to make these trips actually happen. Do you need to save money for the trips? Do you need to ask for the time off work or delegate responsibilities in your business or at home? What about improving on a hobby or sport, such as cycling, sailing or scuba diving? Also, consider a goal you want to achieve and have the trip as a reward!

In the future, you can add to the pages with trips you may not yet know you will be taking or who you will be traveling with. You'll also want to go back to the pages after your adventure and journal about the high points of your trip, treasured memories and final thoughts.

HELPFUL TIP

Print out the last three pages and put them within a dedicated binder. Print one copy of the Master Travel Bucket List and 10 of the Individual Trip pages. Make a cover page with a picture of your first dream destination. Give your trip planner the attention it deserves!

Venice, Italy.
Photo by
Marco Secchi

Brainstorm
For your next trip, what action steps do you need to accomplish?

Photo by Salty Wings

Set Deadlines and Move Forward

Don't stop now. You're almost finished!

> You've made great progress in building your travel bucket list and have begun to outline your travel goals. The next step is to make it all happen with a solid travel plan for the upcoming trips.

Some trips and destinations take more time to plan than others.

For a nearby weekend ski trip, you may only need a few weeks to plan. A cruise is best planned six to 14 months in advance. An African safari needs more like 18 months.

You will need to decide when to start planning the details of your first and second trips. And if you will do all the research and booking yourself, or if you will benefit from the help of a travel advisor.

Keep in mind that the average "do it yourself" traveler spends about 30 hours of research before booking their trip. Not to mention, they run themselves about 30 percent over budget! On the other hand, advisors have the expertise, experience and connections to sort through options quickly, and secure the best value for your money.

Do you think you might want to go at it alone with the travel planning process?

Consider the following scenario:

Let's say your goal is to visit an elephant sanctuary in Thailand. We can break down the planning process into the following steps:

New York, United States. Photo by Denys Nevozhai

- Research best time for Thailand travel
- Research different areas of Thailand
- Find locations of well-respected elephant sanctuaries
- Plan a budget
- Find a hotel in the area of the sanctuary
- Research flights to Thailand
- Research local tours and activities
- Plan other excursions
- Research transportation methods from and to the airport
- Research travel insurance
- Look into getting Global Entry
- Renew passport and look up visa requirements
- Build an itinerary
- Research any vaccinations or other medical prerequisites
- Call credit card companies to make aware of out-of-country travel
- Exchange currency
- Confirm all reservations
- Print all travel documents

MORE FREE GIFTS!

For a free, printable travel planning kit, head over to luxuristtravel.com/planner

For the free Virtuoso Wanderlist® trip planner app, head to luxuristtravel.com/wanderlist

REFLECTION

How will you plan each trip?

The Benefits of Using a Travel Advisor

I can't stress enough the benefits of using a travel advisor.

Whether or not you work with me specifically, a good advisor is a valuable asset. An important part of an advisor's business is to be familiar with the destinations they promote. We travel and check the hotels, talk with the tour guides, go on the excursions, etc., to make sure the quality is as advertised. We talk to sales representatives and each other to verify what we don't know for sure. If you are trusting an old picture online or a review of someone who you don't know, you might be in for an awful surprise. It is one of the paradoxes of our Internet age that, with ever more information at our fingertips, there is also more misleading (or false) information masquerading online. And believe me, it can fool even seasoned travelers.

I hear more and more complaints from travelers who believe they were willfully misled on their last vacation. Then they come to me, the travel advisor, who knows exactly what the destination and the accommodation is like. My job is to ensure you experience the vacation you and your family have been visualizing, something that will be very special and create awesome memories. And this involves listening to your dreams then developing them through conscientious planning. Travel advisors want to know you and how you like to travel, and can custom-design your dream vacations. And they take care of you before, during and after your trip.

When the Covid-19 virus provoked an international travel ban in the spring of 2020, I spent many hours booking some clients on immediate flights home. For months, I kept all my clients informed of upcoming cancellations and rescheduling policies. I even negotiated with vendors for refunds versus credits. I also cancelled their reservations or rebooked everything for them. Other travelers who had booked on their own or through large online booking engines had no one to advocate for them and could not get through to reach anyone at customer service.

When travel surged again in September 2020, I was booking tons of last-minute vacations. Destinations were opening up every day and each had their own regulations. I kept track of that for everyone and posted important updates to my Facebook followers and newsletter subscribers. Many airlines continued to consolidate their flights, which meant lots of schedule changes. Several of these changes were not at all convenient (like an eight-hour layover), so I got back on the phone again, requesting refunds for flights to rebook my clients on other airlines. These things take a lot of time and again, the clout of a large host agency helps. It pays to have a professional travel advisor on your side.

Or, if you want the best possible service, contact me!

Estee Gubbay | Luxury Travel Specialist

- Estee@LuxuristTravel.com
- +1 858-381-7713
- facebook.com/LuxuristTravelAgency
- luxuristtravel.com
- Instagram/LuxuristTravel

Luxurist Travel is a proud member of Virtuoso®, a network of the world's finest travel advisors and suppliers.

A Virtuoso® travel advisor can add a lot of value to your travel:

We can help you get upgrades and extra benefits you'd never be able to secure on your own. Typically, that means room or cabin upgrades, free breakfasts, resort credits, early check-in/late checkout and extra amenities! You can't VIP yourself, and not every advisor does this, but I love calling up hotel managers and telling them how important my clients are and asking what we can do to make their stay more special. Those upgrades also take your vacation to another level of luxury.

We will give you extra insight from our own extensive travels. I scout hotels, build relationships with guides, find the best restaurants, and more. I am also a luxury traveler. My family's favorite hotel brands are Montage®, Four Seasons® and The One and Only®. I know what you expect in high-end travel.

We get to know you personally so that they can help you plan a customized trip. We plan trips tailored to your unique interests and not just what's promoted on the Internet. Advisors help you expand your horizons and imagine even grander, more amazing experiences than you might have known were possible.

We can leverage our relationships with preferred vendors to get the best offers and packages. These are the sorts of opportunities you simply won't find through an online booking engine. There is great value in this. Think about it this way... You call a hotel, cruise line or tour to book directly and you are one customer to them. That doesn't hold a lot of clout. It's far better for your travel advisor to leverage the hotel's relationship with their travel consortium. The hotel has to be invited as members based on their quality of service and many other factors. It's very important to keep their consortium customers happy.

ADVISOR TIP

Even after you've begun your dream trip, advisors represent you & can be your "fixer".

ESTEE'S EXAMPLE

I regularly encounter clients who tell me how, having booked a vacation in a destination marketed as a veritable Shangri-la, they arrived to find a real difference between the location and what was advertised. The most infamous of these was the 2017 Fyre Festival: Fyre was marketed on Instagram as a long weekend event that would be many things: the best music festival in the world, held on a beautiful island in the Bahamas with luxury accommodations, promoted by and packed with influencers, super models, athletes, DJs and rappers. As you can imagine, the prices charged to go to Fyre were high. Yet the thousands of people who paid large sums to go and party at this supposed Caribbean paradise found a scrubby island bereft of everything promised. Even running water was a luxury. Fyre turned out to be an expensive scam. Obviously, Fyre Festival is a pretty extreme example, but it's worth remembering that there are charlatans who will attempt to sell you the travel experience of your dreams (which then turn out to be nightmares).

Dam Square,
Amsterdam,
Netherlands.
Photo by
redcharlie

Conclusion
Congratulations on completing this guide!

> You're now well on your way to making your travel dreams a reality. But don't put this book down for good. Keep tweaking your responses and jot down ideas. Amend when you are inspired. Reevaluate after each of your trips. As you travel, take notes on what experiences are making you the happiest. Can you incorporate more of these or is there something new you would like to try?

At times, this guide might have seemed like a bit of work; planning meaningful travel does require effort. While, other times, it was likely a lot of fun; imagining yourself doing exciting things in destinations you've dreamed about for years is thrilling! Collectively, I'd bet you and your traveling companions gained some important insights and sparked new life into old dreams! The best part is that, together, the work and fun you've had here will pay off by awarding you with travel that inspires lasting, meaningful and life-long impressions.

So now that you have made it this far, what's next?

Keep inspired! If you would like more support, below are a couple of steps you can follow.

Wherever you go next, I wish you all the best. May you dream big, take action and live an amazing life.

Estee Gubbay

Here are a couple of steps

❶ Subscribe to the free Virtuoso® Traveler Magazine and receive the limited edition Best of the Best in Travel book by subscribing at luxuristtravel.com

❷ Join my private, online Facebook group of travelers, where you will be coached in the process of filling out your bucket list at facebook.com/luxuristtravelagency

❸ To receive all the free gifts I offered in this book and more, go to luxuristtravel.com/reader-gifts

❹ If this book has inspired you, I'd appreciate it if you could leave a review on Amazon to let others know.

Falkertsee,
Austria. Photo by
Michael Niessl

6
Your Travel Bucket List Worksheets

Master Travel Bucket List

DESTINATION	ACTIVITY	DATE	COMPLETED

Tylösand, Halmstad, Suède. Photo by Storiès

Master Travel Bucket List

DESTINATION	ACTIVITY	DATE	COMPLETED

Bucket List Trip

Name: ....

DESTINATION	ACTIVITY	TRAVEL TYPE	ACCOMMODATION	DEPARTURE/ RETURN DATE

I want to do this because:

....

....

....

....

Memories I hope to create are:

....

....

....

....

Some things I hope to learn more about:

....

....

....

....

....

Who I want to come with us:

....

....

....

To make this happen I need to:

....

....

....

What were the high points, treasured memories and thoughts?

....

....

....

....

....

....

Review after trip is completed:

Bucket List Trip

Name:..

DESTINATION	ACTIVITY	TRAVEL TYPE	ACCOMMODATION	DEPARTURE/ RETURN DATE

I want to do this because:

....

....

....

....

Memories I hope to create are:

....

....

....

....

Hotel Ses Fotges, Platja de Muro, Spain. Photo by Linus Nylund

Some things I hope to learn more about:

....
....
....
....
....
....

Who I want to come with us:

....
....
....

To make this happen I need to:

....
....
....

What were the high points, treasured memories and thoughts?

....
....
....
....
....
....

Review after trip is completed:

Bucket List Trip

Name: ....

DESTINATION	ACTIVITY	TRAVEL TYPE	ACCOMMODATION	DEPARTURE/ RETURN DATE

I want to do this because:

....

....

....

....

Memories I hope to create are:

....

....

....

....

Photo by Chris Lawton

Some things I hope to learn more about:

....
....
....
....
....
....

Who I want to come with us:

....
....
....

To make this happen I need to:

....
....
....

What were the high points, treasured memories and thoughts?

....
....
....
....
....
....
....

Review after trip is completed:

Bucket List Trip

Name: ....

DESTINATION	ACTIVITY	TRAVEL TYPE	ACCOMMODATION	DEPARTURE/ RETURN DATE

I want to do this because:

....

....

....

....

Memories I hope to create are:

....

....

....

....

Some things I hope to learn more about:

....

....

....

....

....

....

Who I want to come with us:

....

....

....

To make this happen I need to:

....

....

....

What were the high points, treasured memories and thoughts?

Review after trip is completed:

....

....

....

....

....

....

Bucket List Trip

Name:..

DESTINATION	ACTIVITY	TRAVEL TYPE	ACCOMMODATION	DEPARTURE/ RETURN DATE

I want to do this because:

....

....

....

....

Memories I hope to create are:

....

....

....

....

Hotel Ses Fotges, Platja de Muro, Spain. Photo by Linus Nylund

Some things I hope to learn more about:

....

....

....

....

....

....

Who I want to come with us:

....

....

....

To make this happen I need to:

....

....

....

What were the high points, treasured memories and thoughts?

....

....

....

....

....

....

Review after trip is completed:

Bucket List Trip

Name:...

DESTINATION	ACTIVITY	TRAVEL TYPE	ACCOMMODATION	DEPARTURE/ RETURN DATE

I want to do this because:

....

....

....

....

Memories I hope to create are:

....

....

....

....

Photo by Chris Lawton

Some things I hope to learn more about:

....

....

....

....

....

....

Who I want to come with us:

....

....

....

To make this happen I need to:

....

....

....

What were the high points, treasured memories and thoughts?

Review
after trip is
completed:

....

....

....

....

....

....

Made in the USA
Monee, IL
13 May 2022

96354263R00071